MOTHER

MAYA ANGELOU

MOTHER

A Cradle to Hold Me

RANDOM HOUSE | NEW YORK

MOTHER

It is true

I was created in you.

It is also true

That you were created for me.

I owned your voice.

It was shaped and tuned to soothe me.

Your arms were molded

Into a cradle to hold me, to rock me.

The scent of your body was the air

Perfumed for me to breathe.

Mother,
During those early, dearest days
I did not dream that you had
A large life which included me,
For I had a life
Which was only you.

Time passed steadily and drew us apart.

I was unwilling.

I feared if I let you go

You would leave me eternally.

You smiled at my fears, saying

I could not stay in your lap forever

That one day you would have to stand

And where would I be?

You smiled again.

I did not.

Without warning you left me,

But you returned immediately.

You left again and returned,

I admit, quickly,

But relief did not rest with me easily.

You left again, but again returned.

You left again, but again returned.

Each time you reentered my world

You brought assurance.

Slowly I gained confidence.

You thought you knew me,

But I did know you,

You thought you were watching me,

But I did hold you securely in my sight,

Recording every moment,

Memorizing your smiles, tracing your frowns.

In your absence

I rehearsed you,

The way you had of singing

On a breeze,

While a sob lay

At the root of your song.

The way you posed your head
So that the light could caress your face
When you put your fingers on my hand
And your hand on my arm,
I was struck with a sense of health,
Of strength and very good fortune.

You were always
The heart of happiness to me,
Bringing nougats of glee,
Sweets of open laughter.

During the years when you knew nothing
And I knew everything, I loved you still.
Condescendingly of course,
From my high perch
Of teenage wisdom.
I grew older and
Was stunned to find
How much knowledge you had gleaned,
And so quickly.

Mother I have learned enough now
To know I have learned nearly nothing.
On this day
When mothers are being honored,
Let me thank you
That my selfishness, ignorance, and mockery
Did not bring you to
Discard me like a broken doll
Which had lost its favor.
I thank you that
You still find something in me
To cherish, to admire, and to love.

I thank you, Mother.
I love you.

ABOUT THE AUTHOR

Poet, writer, performer, teacher, and director MAYA ANGELOU was raised in Stamps, Arkansas, and then moved to San Francisco. In addition to her bestselling autobiographies, beginning with *I Know Why the Caged Bird Sings,* she has also written a cookbook, *Hallelujah! The Welcome Table;* five poetry collections, including *I Shall Not Be Moved* and *Shaker, Why Don't You Sing?;* and the celebrated poem "On the Pulse of Morning," which she read at the inauguration of President William Jefferson Clinton, and "A Brave and Startling Truth," written at the request of the United Nations and read at its fiftieth anniversary. Her poem "Amazing Peace" was read at the lighting of the National Christmas Tree in December 2005.

Copyright © 2006 by Maya Angelou

All rights reserved.

Published in the United States by Random House,
an imprint of The Random House Publishing Group,
a division of Random House, Inc., New York.

RANDOM HOUSE and colophon are registered
trademarks of Random House, Inc.

ISBN 1-4000-6601-8

Printed in the United States of America on acid-free paper

www.atrandom.com

2 4 6 8 9 7 5 3 1

First Edition